ALSO BY JOHN ASHBERY

POETRY

Turandot and Other Poems

Some Trees

The Tennis Court Oath

Rivers and Mountains

The Double Dream of Spring

Three Poems

The Vermont Notebook

Self-Portrait in a Convex Mirror

Houseboat Days

As We Know

Shadow Train

A Wave

Selected Poems

April Galleons

Flow Chart

Hotel Lautréamont

And the Stars Were Shining

Can You Hear, Bird

Wakefulness

The Mooring of Starting Out:
The First Five Books of Poetry

Girls on the Run

Your Name Here

As Umbrellas Follow Rain

Chinese Whispers

Where Shall I Wander

A Worldly Country

Notes from the Air:
Selected Later Poems

Collected Poems, 1956–1987

Planisphere

Quick Question

Breezeway

FICTION

A Nest of Ninnies
(with James Schuyler)

PLAYS

Three Plays

CRITICISM AND ESSAYS

Reported Sightings:
Art Chronicles, 1957–1987

Other Traditions (The Charles
Eliot Norton Lectures)

Selected Prose

COMMOTION OF THE BIRDS

COMMOTION

NEW POEMS BY

OF THE BIRDS

JOHN ASHBERY

ecco

An Imprint of HarperCollinsPublishers

HarperCollins books may be purchased for educational, business,
or sales promotional use. For information, please email the
Special Markets Department at SPsales@harpercollins.com.

Ecco® and HarperCollins® are trademarks of HarperCollins Publishers.

FIRST EDITION

Designed by Quemadura
This book is printed on Earthchoice Tradebook Freesheet

Library of Congress Cataloging-in-Publication Data has been applied for.

ISBN 978-0-06-256509-9

16 17 18 19 20   QK/RRD   10 9 8 7 6 5 4 3 2 1

FOR DAVID, AGAIN

COMMOTION OF THE BIRDS

We're moving right along through the seventeenth century.
The latter part is fine, much more modern
than the earlier part. Now we have Restoration Comedy.
Webster and Shakespeare and Corneille were fine
for their time but not modern enough,
though an improvement over the sixteenth century
of Henry VIII, Lassus and Petrus Christus, who, paradoxically,
seem more modern than their immediate successors,
Tyndale, Moroni, and Luca Marenzio among them.
Often it's a question of seeming rather than being modern.
Seeming is almost as good as being, sometimes,
and occasionally just as good. Whether it can ever be better
is a question best left to philosophers
and others of their ilk, who know things
in a way others cannot, even though the things
are often almost the same as the things we know.
We know, for instance, how Carissimi influenced Charpentier,
measured propositions with a loop at the end of them
that brings things back to the beginning, only a little
higher up. The loop is Italian,
imported to the court of France and first despised,

then accepted without any acknowledgment of where
it came from, as the French are wont to do.
It may be that some recognize it
in its new guise—that can be put off
till another century, when historians
will claim it all happened normally, as a result of history.
(The baroque has a way of tumbling out at us
when we thought it had been safely stowed away.
The classical ignores it, or doesn't mind too much.
It has other things on its mind, of lesser import,
it turns out.) Still, we are right to grow with it,
looking forward impatiently to modernism, when
everything will work out for the better, somehow.
Until then it's better to indulge our tastes
in whatever feels right for them: this shoe,
that strap, will come to seem useful one day
when modernism's thoughtful presence is installed
all around, like the remnants of a construction project.
It's good to be modern if you can stand it.
It's like being left out in the rain, and coming
to understand that you were always this way: modern,
wet, abandoned, though with that special intuition
that makes you realize you weren't meant to be
somebody else, for whom the makers
of modernism will stand inspection
even as they wither and fade in today's glare.

PRAYER NOT TO TOUCH

Unwillingly, O queen, I left your shore.
Bleeding today, I need you to work with him.
It was the summer of long pants and locusts.
Few could abide his storming at them, none
tried to escape. It was only natural to shrug off
the latest mingled warning, as though it were a commercial
for cake mix.
                    One, foxier than the rest,
perceived a rest in the order for that evening.
Chickens were running around, but it was the stricture
between heel and toe that captured the gripe water
crystallinely. It wasn't your fault, you see,
that a single potato emerged from the vast how-to library.
The others had long since cashed in their chips and traipsed
homeward. Fear was a small flare on the horizon.

I tell you, it was then I knew you were chasing me,
mockery on your lip during the morning meet-and-greet.
Others than I saw the vast
punch pushing love up toward the surface. To do nothing
was our ancient privilege. And though we'd talked about it later,

it always felt unacknowledged, as though we never met,
only passed each other in some narrow alley, where brushing
against one's neighbor was unavoidable, not putrid.

The four-foot hero sandwich says, "I'm here!"
Dozens of golden canaries bask in the receptacle
its loose panniers provided. And all right, I said I
wouldn't do it if I was him. We quarreled and separated
as though forever. And a warm feeling
came to replace that other receptacle of pain,
the long-lounging postmark, from the mountains that summer.

FEATURETTE

Do not fear the gulches
asleep on the farm. It didn't die like that.

Don't go buying anything
and go do something. And very tired, dog-tired,
sometimes I think we were better off
before all the new inventions—the trompe-l'oeil fried egg,
the American flea. I didn't die like that.
This is how we usually
                    yes it is too like that

get it on . . .
Much of this has little to do
with how we shaved and behaved,
                              or mixed doubles.

You're right, the gargantuan sales are over.
I guess my question (a humble bricklayer) is
kiss it and make it go away; the comedy-on-the-train operetta,
a huge success when it opened in Shanghai,

sewn right-leg to right-leg.
Life is a short short story
with explosive simmering.

Who else d'ya like in poetry?
We didn't have time for lunch.
Be ready to hug your glass star.
I'd advise you to.
Are you scorpion enough to even try?
No-good green parents accrue in fives.
He doesn't want to do it himself, then
beautiful, and happy
under a coat of vanish, er, varnish.
(Not in pharmacies) it went viral.

TALES FROM SHAKESPEARE

It seemed like a huge part of our lives
revolved around the woodpile, all buzz
and splatter one minute, low wigwams the next.

He made a horse, like what was on the farm
at which end of the store they let
the young men practice. (The others dress funny.)
Kids used to hang around, lowering the bar for

the vanilla tower

following its pipsqueak editor out
into the brilliant day, of casings, undeliverable, unprogrammed
appliance scepters, more. High bleachers shut off
a section of downtown. It's a part of France,

but I don't drink at these fountains.

His preceptor writes back and
thick as the dust on these reports (that's
my definition anyway, all enthusiastic,

or do we have to be
or does it matter?):
Welcome to the family tree.
I am sick and tired. Startling hog
ends up in a commercial
out of the bathroom window. Thanks for the soda, Pop,
and digital power. Been wondering what it was.

It was time for the rectory bells, balls, whatever.
It seemed like it to me, too. The reply
to her demandingness.

Somebody sends you a bill.
At first you want to laugh. Who said
that everything was going to be a thrill?
Just leave it. The little puffin on the green-
house steps turned around,
annoyed with everything.

OK, let's cope.

THE UNDERLING

It's very exciting to walk along,
follow these with interesting things,
and get to spend time mostly in Europe
in my July pants.

Though we could sign off, the lesbian anchor
wants to say something. So how are you?
Our daily stump, guy getting ready to eat one,
husbands at a time,
horse removal.
And, arbitrator, he talks about you,
pokes around in the refrigeration
where all is tickety boo, the larches
(all of which are favorable enough),

the darker haired mechanisms,
the worker mnemonic—
Hi, Mnemosyne (running episode
or lived something like that,
entangled lead for the peacekeepers),

because after 200 years the youngster'd
want some tomalley.
But, maybe *after* that . . .
he could take up cooking—
braised sunchokes, coils included.

How did you hear about themselves?
She remembered huh. That's what it's for.
Adult dolphins, swingeing along . . .
I'll put you up on the wall, then
make it home for the first time.
And he was probably gonna hurt himself
on the folded glass doors. She must be having another,
and we could have a big conversation
or any big sporting group, regular dancers.
His lesions were legion.

WHO WILL DO THE KISSING?

You will not have heard that.
What about the leftover duck?
Who will do the kissing?
They have gone ice skating.

RAINBOW LAUNDRY

At Opium Bridge
an apple with orange signature.

No but a cat came in,
rushing around as though its life depended on it

and lets you deal with
all of that.

Just remember the Red River Valley, that's
all I ask,

the color sergeant said.

LATE-ISH

The girl in the green ski chasuble
hasn't yet graduated from radio school.
Let's pay attention.

Looking ahead, why, he waved his mouth along.
Doesn't life get difficult in the summer?
The divine medicine for it collapsed
in front of the shortstop,
who took off like a battalion.

Crowds of older people who would read this
happily, willingly, then walking into night's embrace,
then kiss. *"To turn you out, to turn you out!"*
Sometimes an arm is accused:
You could have felt it, the blue shirts,
phlegm central, four times a night.
But what does that get me?
Light refreshments.

When the suburban demonstration kind of shrunk
you put your foot out,

leave it or kiss it
or even two years ago,
Charmaine here tells us.
I think I should stay . . .

Cross-eyed sonofabitch . . .
He liked him, he could tell. A de-happening.
The gangster no longer wanted to sleep with him,
but what the heck. With time off
for actual fuzz collected . . . All right, boys.
Cheap murders, peach driven . . . I seen enough of those
samples along the way.

THE HAPPY QUESTIONER

It isn't very late,
and that probably won't come as a surprise.
I found out where I probably was last summer.
That was supposed to mean something,
and then we might have been misunderstood.

. . . didn't spend the night.
You don't see as much thermos.
Terrorists jumped the gun
too often down there, home to the Squishy Mountains,
sex in a cave. All the feelings of the current machine.
Crazy mud houses, not purchased here.
He has the same long bottle of thanks sent to the newsroom,
or both. Nor was the defense urgent,
or whether April 7. That has come about,
ready to be ridiculed—
Bill, and his cat,
her grocery and all,
my cargo dress
just so I'll know.

Crossing the international sinuses,
we're hurting. Take it out of your system
and march. Or fill the lower car.
Get the sacred juices flowing!

Some houses aren't empirical.
How does that make it a regular object?
Now. No. Not on this side.

She has active breasts and a history of sleeping disorders
in the nainsook nighties of contradict and beyond.

A FUNNY DREAM

His aunt was accepted.
How cool is that?

A new desire,
plainer than I can doubt
lightens the cities of the plain.

All is effulgent, sawtooth fronds,
veiled undertones.
Then the question remains: What is it?

Leaving his shorts behind, he
hastened to rejoin the marchers up ahead—
a peanut pastime, pleats, tucks, and panels,
unreinforced paint thinner.

So turn this off.

THE OLD SOFA

Hello. I have to go
in a little while. Well,
maybe later. If at all.

There hasn't been better than the average atmosphere.
After dinner we're turning all the lamps into magic lanterns.
We'll see who knows best.

The camera began taking pictures.
If they'd like some again, after the day
after tomorrow, they can have it.

One genius throttles two or more. I know. Tell them I
said it. And they kill . . . and kill . . .
Beetles don't count any more. If you hadn't seen one . . .

The stage splashed with finishing light.

Take a family of fish. Grandpa,
grandma, a school of pickerel and
two uncles. What life's about . . .

Eat your victuals. Company is coming,
with the audience primed for the invasion series.
What more could I expect from longing?

This season's layered look resembles last
year's, in that both are harried.
Two or more were wanting.

The shades are drawn earlier, as light expands
always when a productive air settles over the terrain.
Buy philological figs.

Friends . . . die down with me.
Shouldna done that. House passed away.
I'm taking the lunatic express. House passed away
in two different cities. Manny's propaganda film

if she would have done,
insisted they have no place
(and that's another thing about it).
That should tell you something.

THE NATIONAL DEBT

We bought the pudding close to the ground
for the mewling sound its creases make.
But there was another coming up, the goddess fixture
from whom no reckoning was assuaged. Ah,
the mathematics of earlier tea times.
And when he had sung into it, why,
it was useless to assert valid countervalences.
Yes, that was only for nobles
in the golden chamber. Starshine and a few good
fallen breezes, to remind us where else we were at.

Meanwhile I was pleasured.
Alternate forms of transport
brought surf to the eyelids,
will be provided those unlucky enough
to find themselves in such a position
that time tomorrow.

Pretty happy at times,
is that why we all got paid money?

I can be bought,
the weight of my hair shimmers,
recalling something back from the distant future,
something we'd like, and which likes us . . .
Scheherazade! Was it you all along? Then why
did that other landfill clamor for remainders
that heaven had seen fit to dole out, to us,
quietly undeserving, as best it can?

Do you have a favorite magazine?
Do you consider yourself left-wing?
High maintenance? The content gets to be
infected, or slips out of focus.
Workmen install the fish vulgate.

THE ANXIOUS MUSIC

Everybody and his BFF was there.
It doesn't get much sweeter than this,
O churlish associate. "Dink," I said,
"This was something they kept appraising."

No snow in just anyone's car.
Though too much literature is a bad thing,
you have to live with that. You sing really good
(as if he'd ever be enough for his birthday)!

AS SOMEONE WHO LIKES TRAVEL

The climate is pretty.
I wrote everything on it.
That's the activity where it
gets relatively inauspicious.

They all got your email,
looking presidential
or not.

I've been meaning to pick up a bag of lettuce on my way home.
This is the thing that I needed,
where he relates.
On an emulsion? Well, there are worse things to
build on. 'Cause I'm not going to.

What's it supposed to be of?
Why so many engineered? The account
is unreceivable. People also look for
"just not rollicking." Which is my advice to you
in my capacity as "can't do that any more."

It was OK but it was hurting.
Norma Face Card offered a million but you had to
wear contrasting piping.

And you were sitting there
in the night of life. It sure was good.
My favorite desserts were there.
And when they invite you, it's like an important document
goes missing. I'll give you an example:
a twelve-year struggle upstate, in
the slick atmosphere of the breakfast room.
It might have gotten stuck in her farthingale.

Otherwise no reply.

DANGEROUS ASYLUM

As famous as a broken disc,
thanks for coming all this way.
That's why I have to do it,
to be a goon that matters
into another person's life.

You have a lousy voice, but
a good tenor. There, I've said it.
You'll have to quickly get back
on the job, brothers brothers.
In her transparent hair
she is, well, just a person,
Bruce confessed.

And that stuff is now getting cold.
I'll be there for you;
they want to cut them off from other
poppy-seed cakes,
getting—getting old again,

frustrated bobby soxer.

Hold that opera—you made the lyrics.

You remind me of you.

We had been up to Speculator once before.

Off you go then.

BELEAGUERED

Lacking a better term for it
your boyfriend's boyfriend opens out to
a large plastic bag northbound, with
northern nuances, disturbed and impressed
by one still kept in conversations,
though fled beyond advantage.
You might want to do it again.
There's a lot you don't know, hey hum.

BUT NOBODY SAYS SO

So we just mighta snapped it off. It came served with toast points. I mean it was kind of golden. In receding rays. Git gracious if you know what I mean, which you most assuredly don't. Aha, I glimpsed you that one time in the recording booth. This was as modern as it had ever been. They were influenced by him. Some dirty magazine prodded the water pistol duo.

Get up and laugh, investigate or communicate. It's only your future after all. It's not like you were the only person to have ever had fantasies. The S & M's weren't all that knowledgeable, or sure. Besides others come out of the ground at all moments, determined to blot your lipstick into something more gay and manageable.

So it was the spare root, not the square root. I told you so all along. Get up and laugh, investigate or communicate. It doesn't matter which. What does matter is the sloshing sound that can be heard around its stump. Nobody wants to deal with that. Likewise, all came here under the sheltering palm fronds so's to be around. So take your sex kit and be off with you. In other words hang around all day until the golden toast buds slide across the washboard surface like honey across waffles. That is the day we shall meet. I hope to heck it comes soon. You'll soon see the advantages of a puckered surface, like seersucker on the moon.

FOOD EPISODE

Body, what do you think?
To have been a right to know
and colored like Elizabeth . . .
We porched around th' unpopulated air
and grassy ornament. Your gallery,
O wondrous cloud, is empty.
What's going on up here?

You'd cup their hands, but I'm
like this cat here—make very serious activity
too long ago, half thinking
of what the X—— are able to achieve.
In the Shetland navy
wife takes his things
and clean armpits and assuages
the clean mud.

HILLBILLY AIRS AND DANCES

The same ideas or different ones condense,
and you don't have to sleep again.
Garbage is necessary. That's another issue
that hasn't been talked about.

I hear what you're saying.
Now all together: Everyone is standing
outside some movement: French spenders,
my business train, jillions
of irregular plurals. Like we were all
gone together at some point,
something one could understand,

to confront you with our country,
smoking cloud,

vintage treat, village street.
The other is all mind.
In world aesthetics, a bundle in the straw.

A SEPARATE INCIDENT

Burdick has come through. It
wasn't easy, or, apparently, that
difficult. He and his mother are
without, that is to say, within.
Bobby and Priscilla . . .
                              would you
finish his poem for him?

Here endeth the first lesson,

TEXT TREK

If you say so, "boss," I'll retract my statement.
Only I wouldn't be so radiant if I was you.
The ripple effect, strength in deterioration,
has expanded on more than a handful.

                                        Have a good time,
just get out of the hurricane entrance. I'll see you
there on all fives, explains Lucy.
A face named Al remarked on the long destiny
between veils, where nobody noodles too long
anyway. Less remarked on is the mask-laden buffet.
Angels wash their faces. Lady Godiva for one.

Leave some room for the astonishingly mild
ripple-effect milkweed fence. And say, once that has
lapsed, go on a trip right now. Don't we have to register?
A slow branch is to be beheaded. Old trash,
what somebody said half a million times,
chimes farther down in the seat.

Unhouse the birds. Make your time over there
a ribald heraldry of number-coaching animals,
better early than never. Why, I thought so.
I was right about the comet
and the cement plant fluke, subway Grandma.

UNDERSTANDABLY

It's beautiful, and all that:
the corner student with the carpet tunnel
or you just don't know
where to get one
which is all that matters.
I didn't know but what
during our recent homecoming special
very good plastic muffins were featured,
(the cement trees yesterday),

and that probably wouldn't be a surprise.
Turn the window off.
The stars, what happens next?
Replacement issues, timid leftovers
burning in reality.

Bear with me, bears.
The radar committee (woman in bathrobe, man
in bad mood) backed down. The chosen honorees arose
or are you going up? I don't sit with smaller operations.

The ant farm, tossed on frozen seas—
didn't they have an old pinup of yours?
The hairnet (stay away) protects my great big head.
In your smart capacity summon the ambassador.
And the infection? It grew.
In 1951 I really, really am, little chum.
Sorry about the vegetables. Stones'll be pretty with that.

What do you want, John? Informally, a
new body, and an assistant.
I'll bet the place is swarming with printers.
I wrote them yesterday. Really reached out,
plugnutty. Like the noiseless farts of antiquity
squeamishness is best, yet still.

DIE MEISTERSINGER

Only those who actively dislike poetry didn't like him. The others could care less. There were too many other things to worry about, like is my license expired yet? Fortunately there were a few in between, those who school themselves to take an interest in everything, which is not to say they're not truly, deeply interested in the things that matter most. To them he was a special case, something to take home and place on the library mantel, and talk about. To them he was truly unique, like the first in what would become a memorable series.

Mostly these were opera lovers, lovers of all opera, whether by Verdi, Wagner, Gluck or Puccini. They adored this category, which to them was almost as a false religion, something that would have repercussions later but now we are enjoying it with no regrets, like a freshly cooked fish. And so he got off lightly, amid the ceremony of unsnapping pyramid-folded dinner napkins and making conversation about trivial subjects, the better to enjoy the illicit feast that was rolling down the rails toward them. "You'll be my fancy, won't you?" Yes indeed, once I polish off this ephemeral morsel. Then we'll all be more or less part of the conversation, which will lead to enlightenment.

Not so fast, though. He was raising himself, like a pudding on a platter. "You guys know where you are? I'm trying to figure out what in hell's going on. So is he too," he added, waving his fork at the piebald host, who pressed a napkin to his exquisite lip.

"No need to panic, folks. Our friend is but the first in a series that may well turn out to be infinite, if past experience is any indicator."

The clock is running over, and an octopus wears my wallet now.

STRANGERS MAY KISS

It wouldn't be the first time (either),
curvaceous, some of the art work
keeps spilling, and so on.

Don't say anything.
(You always need to get somewhere,
civil engine,
some more dumb bunny cheesecake.)
Thanks for having me
slipshod and enjoy
his undistinguished underwear.

Literary schools and manners
was not mistaken about his
it got that way just the end
not after eleven o'clock at night,
chubby accent.

Fact: I'm tempted to sort of slither in its path,
all that rot.
Where you going to hang it from?

Yes I suppose so and
I want you to get another one of those
from apparent disorder but
but kind of
even drink to this.
You probably won't see us again.

Is it great being uncomfortable there?
We didn't call it that.

WHATEVER THE OLD MAN

DOES IS ALWAYS RIGHT

I

First of all, you aren't telling me the whole story.

Friday saw armpit futures rise across the country.
It is an acknowledged truth that you and your little brother
sidled across a city of two million souls.
Well, and were we supposed to forget it?
That's not the way the soul functions in today's suburbia.

We'll have no more of that, nor go a-roving.

II

All cabbages and cukes are on sale.
That's because there was a rumor of shortages
in the flanks of winter, before we were on the scene

or were of a responsible age. Sure enough, other young adults
will take our place at the helm. Sure, a bitter pill,
multiple corn dogs, and I ask you. Already Fred Flintstone
was having second thoughts. They arrived in the form of tremendous
cloud barriers, rendering all other life sterile
and attractive. Two more is all you get after we're outta here.
You saved us once. This is the result, and our resolve.

III

I saw it and no one believed me. The old man wept quietly.

IV

And there was further loose talk in Maida Vale re the kind
of outsiders you can expect now that the yeoman class is finished.
And lo, one went out from them. "Intuit me, Jesus." And then
the other classes stayed put a certain time before they too set out,
having no permanent idea of the future. Sure enough, supplies
arrived. And were put to good use. But still it was time for more.

V

The old man wouldn't hear of it. Said we all had had enough
of it in our youth, were spoiled rotten. Wait, where's
the evidence of that? If I'm spoiled so be it, but at least let
the aroma of charming decay play over the surfaces. Color me
    shitfaced
if you must, but repay my obloquy in bright coin.
Otherwise the aims and achievements of one side
will always be parallel to the other, and now I bid you good night.
Thus the score was tallied, heavily.

List to all his energy being pulled.
Alarm is a form of handwriting this time. Wash your basement.
This is him doing a moose soup.

VI

Thy tines, thy sediment, swizzling health
that she and a girlfriend grew
of aryan certainty and cockeyed pride, all have been
scratched. I make a 39 percent commission
on our magic spatula,
driving it on four cylinders to the dump.

On the superseded golf course
cherries with Brenda. O their hearts are fantastically gay.
I will.

VII

In Crispy Town
swamp butter, what became our lips,
dear boy . . . old chap, smuggle I mean snuggle
a thank-you note
or my all-night interview, for that matter.
I wonder if my dad's disk can matter
and yes, she didn't write poems
and wanted to check on me.

How could anyone?
I'd love to see—don't give me that.
Dressed to—I can't complain kinky forests, tenuous.
Look at them and decide which one.

Unhappy lumberings in the heart. Tom is ready.
The jerk remedy is working.
You dropped something.
It must have been important, they say.

And girls' volleyball
of six dozen years, as smooth a warranty
as you're likely to snag,
that can blow up suddenly,
a little bit more poignant
to my older sister

straight into the Atlantic.

What is your foot exactly?
Flummoxed . . .
the makeshift western quarter
and I wish I could devalue you a currency.

Where do I first blurt him out?

THIS ONCE

. . . or somebody's going to get hurt.

For my sake, however, keep pealing to a minimum.

We'll need the firewood you can pick up on the shore

of that lake. Oh and by the way . . .

Splurge. And get moving.

WRITTEN WITH A BALLPOINT

How concerned are you with the man who runs it?
Didn't I hope you enjoyed it too?
Now hopefully, first he said I can't.
Nothing succeeds like success,
always something wrong with me, human issues.
Chaste ephemerae. Don't go on that boat.

How long ago would you be with him at his school?

That's ridiculous. That's great.
I can see you running.

Rhythm and blues imploded, not listening.
What a measurable doubt canceled statutes
of limitations, I'm not sure how.
Attila the Hun must not have been available.
Now get down off that lamp.

If you read it in your journals it's true too.
Now pretty much so, the runny impact through cars,

chemical-laced pants in general, not just me
in the morning time, the afternoon hour,
the prawn sisters' dream-sequence
retro vibe. We're already starting to hear from the paper boy.
There was another incident where they had white boots on.
We call them "sea lollipops."

No word on minor injuries.
Some, not all, bled artificial tears,
very nice and fresh,
in a fancy hotel room. Diversity
gets better all the time, yet wound up taking pictures.
They're not talking about us any more.
Moose wandering at home on the ground,
who's going to pay for it? At $250,000 a year?

Elmer and Thelma met cute
on Floating Island. Have that conversation, serial golf putter.
To not have an uncle, more umbrellas for Dad
in my office, though filled with dead bodies. Secretly independent.

Eight years ago, when I was married to a European high school,
an odd thing happened. Allow me
to prefer the old ways, a lotta remembrance,
no place for heavenlies.

You can die watching the army. It isn't like this.
To make a long story short, I just thought, maybe
keep the bed under here missing pieces. Nowhere fast.
I love the routine, as long as we keep doing the same thing
until the door was open.

CARTOON MUSIC

Do I wish none of this happened? Yes.

GOVERNOR ANDREW CUOMO

Why would she have said that,
an undeserving egg, not to die for?
Rainbow pencils retracted.
Next, a group of officials withdrew support
of accident forgiveness, and I'm like
Comrade Fuzzy, my gaydar's
gone berserk the way it messes.

Or say the response is tepid,
or buttered ramekins. Color me brain foolish,
on eye-drops—the history of his hounding. There,
it's not creepy, but it is.

You can't turn away or around from
the birthday table with its *glaces*
getting iconic around the benches notably.
We're supposed to go out for the evening.
David had saved some money

and that stuff is now getting cold.
Within the relative safety
of the parterre it'll make me sick today.
You're not going to have any trouble.
Standard stories of unrest drag on.
Was that a painful moment?

DEPRAVED INDIFFERENCE

it was just a typical mid-sized town
in the middle of nowhere

JAMES TATE,

"Burn Down the Town, No Survivors"

Customize the event, picking at soul scabs,
turning your face optimistically toward the window.
There must be a long biography coming out soon,
leggings to be worn, and so it is that earth
gets turned over, and we all go back into our little houses
for a while, and the land is generous.
                                    At least,
that's the way it would have turned out, if God
or I had any say in the matter. As it fell out,
our leaders met in the azalea patch
in an election year. Outsiders were welcomed in
with wine and cookies, and we all settled down
to the business of the day. Repealing the Stamp Act
was big on everybody's agenda, stamps being

eternally optimistic, as though indebted to someone.
That's my definition, anyway. Or do we have to be,
or does it matter? Meanwhile the Repair Act languishes.

Welcome to the family tree. I am sick and tired
at my earliest convenience. This was supposed to make it easier,
remember? Hopefully his owner wires back and,
thick as the dust on our reports, finds it totally
unacceptable, yet not entirely unknown, queering
the pitch for kids that used to hang around.
Mr Pom from Camp Cute swept by,
but he could foretell the cloying sound of water
in water, haruspicate, start a restaurant. The broken land
was free to be contaminated, again.

ELECTOR

Ooh Whitey Bear said.
The sun is yellow
in what commercial
we're dreaming of size now
lest it get away!

Or if on another Thursday
your credentials dropped by,
sad they came to see you
flushed with the explaining light
of so on.

Thank you to Seattle.
What they charge
you're enjoying them,
you seem to enjoy them.

We've got to make sure the implications are sharper,
and 23rd Ave. convenience flower.
Fido don't know the novel as seen.
Why you serving him? On the air tonight . . .

KIND PERMISSION

Almost tonight, let's not and say we did.
I used to be a slightly handsome boy, then
this happened. It has been likened to an army
of pebbles rolling down. OK, so adhere.
See if that gets us somewhere. By which I mean
over here. Racial smog
in the country of loved ones.

Come in, anyway, anywhere but in the hamper.
It's good, I'll fix it up, lack of full mentorship
the night you were going to stay up late
and I wasn't even a child anymore
with no elastic purse. What's nubian
state flower? In the house and everywhere,
but what does that get me? . . . could you just smell somebody,
tiny breakers hitting the relaxed shore.
You put your foot out.
Leave it or kiss it,
or even two years ago.

MEAN PARTICLES

Sometimes something like a second
washes the base of this street.
The father and his two assistants
are given permission to go.
One of them, a woman, asks, "Why
did we come here in the first place,
to this citadel of dampness?"

Some days are worse than others,
even if we can't believe in them.
But that was never a concern of mine,
reasoned the patient.

Sing, scroll, or never be blasted by us
into marmoreal meaning, or the fist for it.
Kudos to the prince who journeyed here
to negotiate our release, if you can believe it.

You're right. The ballads are retreating
back into the atmosphere.
They won't be coming round again.
Make your peace.

DESERT MOMENTS

We watched his regular camera
until it became nervous.
There were other horns inside for us,
things the pasta brought, never to be paced over.

My gosh! The President of the United States!
Years and years went by like that.
It was impossible to keep track of them.
I'm all about truth, and meaning. In the end
they said they were delighted with what they found.

Circuits are busy. Of course, we're not going to sit here
and wait. I have met you in the small shops,
a large cookie presence. It was "robust."
Save me the czardas

at Puke University.
I'm glad he goes in there.
That was the president, you clucks.
Why is it taking so long?

We might come closer (the eldritch mother's refrain
over 23 years ago).
Oh, that's what that is.
Then suddenly it's forty years later,
and I was like, "Holy shit!
I'm just happy to be alive!"

It's almost like you've done something
totally preppy. Your hands are a little dirty,
though.
Yrs and oblige,
Holofernes J. Crinkleaf.

"Dear Smitten . . ."

A DISSERVICE

Life with its sorrow, life with its tear.
And you know what that means:
the sky in a drawer,

the underwear underworld
on the floor of the moon.
Under the emergency lamps a small panic was growing,
keeping to itself, chiming
ahead of your headlights, wobbly.
You had just gotten so young
it was all I could do to contain you
in the linen dishtowel we kept for that purpose.
The doctor prescribed bed rest.

The cash cow is a going concern,
the intake not dangerous enough
that you folks enjoy.

It's not immortality,
these mechanical trees, alders.
Good to know you're not killing them all yourself
across the street baby.

THE PRESIDENT'S TOENAIL

Why can't everything stay the way
it used to be, O biggest hipster, dolor?
Well I'm doing it aren't I? Yes, but
the bath has long been drawn.

How long it takes I won't need to know.

By the way, they always ask after you.
My brain-children are not in the least acadian.
Yes but I can do it now,
a little bit independent, whatever the
production values turn out to be.
Stuck with his teeth,
O great and slippery one!
Not here, not anyone, to
be like the president's toenail, unperforming!
In the palace of sinister remorse,
to pollute with their cooking,
briefly held,
a school thing. You could use white chocolate.

It was another gentleman.

He doesn't know what I'll do if he gets one.

Hopefully the real acrobat . . .

DOROTHY VERNON OF HADDON HALL

My summer of dubious irony unspooled
like a tatar's vest, more in the breach.
Sure, others wanted to hold hands, but that was their business.
Me and my orator did just fine,
thank you very much. Yet there comes a time
when kisses no longer matter.
Only then, according to some,
do figs emerge from the grotto where winter kept them,
caramels at the ready, knowing now is the one
score to be settled. After that, we'll see.
But as Ulysses said to the Wise Virgins, it is come and past.
Other criminals are waiting.

The only furniture is when I can't.
The garage home fitted yesterday perfectly.
The irony is it just doesn't stop there.

They seemed so beautiful together,
my ward and homeland security.
If these are omens let us pray to bend them.

Otherwise it's back to the American Revolution, and you know
what that was like. Some had mascots and reasons for patronizing
    them.
One, its little asshole raw from Rappahannock ice,
preferred to break off exploratory talks,
recalling ambassadors. See, it ended this way,
with much still at stake
and even more lost to view.

LAND MASS

A certain amount of nowhere,
sutured suitor, in a desert slot machine—
I actually brought my radio down.

Starfriend,
teach the reader a shy grammar
though we could pass off
wants to say something—
so how are you?

Our daily stump, a
guy getting ready to eat one
of confiscated rapture,
husbands at a time
with cool energy.

Yes I suppose so, and
I want you to get another one of these

got what she needed
got what he deserved

so you're comfortable in the chair
splashier and stackier
factory windows
damaged
the boy, a Jesuit
seen in the kitchen
others scroll away

Which side has no water, or too little water,
its heartthrob dictator
come with all the minor tropes of
in sordid dregs,
his "repositioning" of the
the blue guest
the lines under the limes
you stayed there with me

Of course you handed it so well
a rough day
getting on the phone
bee sculptures
fiber building
car surgery

wedding of the painted doll—
Our fish

on a summit
couldn't have been more nicer
the sign in her nipple
so we can lose to every single one of them.

Your doctor should make recommendations
each franchise is different,
hoary admixture
how you were just
look fellas I'm going to be backup here tomorrow night
The Weather Channel

"Don't come in!"
and getting his own feet (on)
Yawn Magazine

So you can just come back up
oracles in wheelchairs,
goat creature
a few/certain occasions
she wants to wait till after we get here
covert meanders

the indifferent breath
late every second of every day . . .

Kids, this is Moloch. He'll be taking over in study hall. I don't
    know what this is.
Stop milking his act.

It always seems
with all the trimmings
honorable business matter
more adventures
sex—having
not a lot.

THE GAY PHILOSOPHER

You're telling me:
chicanery, the moorhen,
the long triple happy fluid,
the orange response.
By golly that tastes good.

And to another land, more shy, in
any case more remote
nights are more reserved now.
By her coif shall she know you . . .
Error: a large sense of ennui,
such as apples, peaches, pears,
moved in as though to shut down the place,
inspissates, gladly, to bear right.

HAUNTED RIDE

Yes, but . . . isn't that the point?
White house, you're not even seein'.
I'll take a rain check on the trees.
They've remembered.
                          Get the new attendant.
Ride the pink palomino. Like any big artist's leg
he wasn't rapturous,
                          only captivated.
Misguided police draped in cheerful Macbeth plaid
remembered never to toll the dying

brilliance of that great ball again,
the lava farm,
th' intrusive handle.

IMPERMEABLE

Finally, alone.
I was asked, are you sure?
Then the spotlight took over, mended
degenerate fences, fixed frost.

Remember, keep things brash,
unprogrammed. Start the dormition
theory an inch above my head.

We'll never have to respond.
Renewal costs said, in a statement:
You don't need to survive.
Just existing would be enough.

Put his legs under it. Put
pants back on, towel and visitor.
Ladle thy grief in Japanese pinstripes.

Hopefully, northern nuances will be spared
this time around. A few of us sitting around
Rick and Amy's, were up half the night
examining selvage, or salvage.

GLITCH

We're back today with mist on a checked shoe.
To the entertainment of the people, the 5th
annual B—— Film Festival *Leona's Empathy*, has
just been announced. By the time that the alleged victim

puts her own daughter in the supermarket,
sapped limbs, and then it became infected, and . . .
Fellow concierges, you will not hurt me if I slam the door.
It's really not good for her to be inside.

If you're driving downtown (I was going to),
anything I can do to help. But this was 24 hours,
we're talking chicken crosswords, love's bodily face.
I'll bring 'em over here. There was this play

when I was a kid. She played an astronaut. I also think
not to bring food in the house. So let him talk about it
in trying to keep up with him, right where a chicken leg came in,
a certain amount of nowhere.

I lowered the volume. The sweets came first, their range
bracing. But what about the grace-notes? Where are my noisettes,
the elder-flower water? As dirt is to the floor,
which is more than can be said for some people.

SITTING AT THE TABLE

In these situations
I'm trying to figure out what is going on.
So is he too. Purged for oversharing,
he launched a partially deflated football
into the stands. The crow went wild.
We'll ski the gorse on our ankles
provided that makes anyone feel better.
If not the cheapest scent availeth not.
We are all captured, out of work,
clinging to spruce dominions.

It wasn't always this way.
Somewhere, ants were taking control
of earth's blistered pulse.
Peanuts were jettisoned from the nacelle
of the montgolfière, all moyenâgeux and thrifty
as it came to be about. I ask only for staples
for my staple gun. This oilcloth throw goes on
in a jiffy. It will protect the surface
of pure sorbet from what accidental storms may throw at it.
Now back to the kitchen.

The patient shepherd, though, had plotted a circumambient
replique to otherness. If indeed
it wasn't meant to be this way, one person
and only one can time the fly it took to get here.
Levels of drudgery dissolve in the saline light
of imperfect cities placed to test you here, on the road to
somewhere even more accidental.
Yes, it's you I'm talking to.

You see, only a few of us made it out alive.
There was concern for others not recorded in the ship's manifest
who were thought to have taken an early flight. Alas,
such was not the case. The sarabande
is finished, kaput. Not that it matters
to spectators eager for anything, and nothing.
As long as you sign the guest book
the great dream can roll on.

PEOPLE BEHAVING BADLY A CONCERN

Aggressive panhandling, public urination, verbal threats,
public nudity and violation of the open container law
followed us down the days, for why
are we here much longer,
or even this long? I ask you
to be civil and not interrupt night's business.

It was "so fun" getting used to you.
They were influenced by him: some prairie magazine
on the air tonight. (Amid the chaos, reports of survivors.)

Didn't the flowers' restoration cat fugue keep spilling,
and like that? It wouldn't be the first time, either.
The pro-taffeta get up and laugh,
investigate or communicate. The night you were
going to stay up late, others will kiss,
and he talks about you, and I don't know what.
Come in, anyway,
and don't lack for tales of the Assertion.

We're talking civilian unrest.

Yes, well, maybe you should take one.

(Do not bite or chew.)

PLAYING IN DARKNESS

The men on top of the hill
launched a new dirt lobby
meant to outstrip the precious,
that is, previous, tentative
by a better than three-to-one margin.

And slightly without you
horrified spectators esteem the rain input.
You would have too crude shelter
of boards circling a central meaning place.

Arrhythmia! You pant. Not by a long
chalk, crotch shot
on a bowling team, English-worthy kebabs.
Let Fido confide, or cough up. I can't
vouch for the clientele, in lockdown mode.
They don't want you there, aporia.

Mrs. Mulligan down the hall broached the topic
long after everyone had gone home
into the night.

THE UPRIGHT PIANO

Did we once go to bed together?
And how was it? I need your help on this one.
Good thing it happened, too—
Intelligence without understanding
is like constant frost, pounding at the temples
until its bargain is overseen. I kid you not.

We "bought into" the ephebe-consciousness scam
that razed our era, and the next one.
What was it about those boys? Some were plain,
others smooth. All enjoyed the sun
for as long as it chose to shine upon them.
But there were texts to be looked to, dark as forests
when the sun shines in central summer.
Nobody did the escaping this time.

Work with your hands a little bit.
You might want to convert yourself
on a scholarship. I'm hoping to live with him.
I can't tell if it's possible. The blood-presence drives
to sleep longer on the couch, as the fair one pines.

Oh averages! It was your story that brought us down,
at the first posts, under green leaves.
Your logic I forswore, even as its wave reached out toward me.
Hard lines. Besides, it's poor form. (Pure form?)

Somebody left their toothbrush on the dance floor.
My understanding, cool from the diagnosis,
is they don't want it to be there.
You mean you're suffering like everybody?
That, and a few more kicks to the groin, means we're finished here.

O idle light! How polished you were at first!
If things darkened afterward, that was no one's fault
except the self-appointed guardians of our civility's,
who nattered on, dense with the realizing it.
We knew it before. So many flowers washed up on the beach
it was pure chaos, or fun. Now it's time to pray.

COOLER TEMPERATURES

My favorite big slum was the matter
if you need to be.
It had a rhythm all its own.
You're the driver. Let's wait a second,

and get moving.
Don't get any on it.
Was I ever! Refrigerate after opening.
I do so want not to be alone,
not after eleven o'clock at night . . .

The ship breaks up . . .

You *look* nice,
giving away like that.
I'll buy you this and buy you that:
a closer look, a nice warm bed
to hide under
in the event that . . .

His majesty is indisposed,
steals the show as quite collectible,
adding insult to injury,
touching but often hilarious.
God and I had a good laugh over that one.

We lived in a suburban rumor mill a century ago,
now and right around the corner from
business thing.
He felt we were alone.
Few pamphleteers or blue gum
as I came from . . .
and they aren't too happy.

It might be here tonight. I'll have to see.
Almost no one needs her light,
ambles away in shambles. Brass epitaph . . .
I'm turning this off tonight,
beautiful anxiety. What I understand is
no death. Fail in the part where
the ship breaks up,
scissored down.

CRIBBAGE, 1954, UTICA

It wasn't his brown sugar corsage
(light, firmly packed) that tipped us off
to the correct running time. That was fixated
in another century, or as
with ice trays dripping from
swollen hands, like us,
only to ask the pardon of a
perimeter, in sandbag heaven.

It was further noticed
that Spot was missing, though the well-house welkin
lay suspiciously undisturbed. Drat!
Aw . . . This is the last time I get
sent out looking for Juicy Fruit or
Black Jack. One out of two is enuf,
and all the ancestors
who tobogganed down behind us
had a use for you! Quicken

or be sidelined with one or
two ward enforcers. And cut
its own poles, minutes ticking merrily.

My darkness camera amazingly
spews energy coupons
even in Arizona.

BUT SERIOUSLY

Do not include anger at the distance
it takes to get from here to the hill of downtown
that bears the sapphire tower.
Others than you have made the trip, and found
little to marvel at once the arriving was over.

Your words hold too much meaning once
they're released. Save an epigram
for the jar. Once it is lapsed
you'll wear it like an endorsement,
jewel that goes nowhere.

All along the creek where we once stood
new ball games are being absorbed
and declassified. Does that matter to us?
Or is it already time to go back in?
On the Waterfront was a good movie. Can we leave it at that?

DAY BUMP

Whether the harborline or the east shoreline
consummated it was nobody's biz until you got there,
eyelids a-shimmer, content with one more dispensation
from blue above. And just like we were saying,
the people began to show some interest
in the mud-choked harbor. It could be summer again
for all anyone in our class knew.
Yeah, that's right. Bumped from our dog-perch,
we'd had to roil with the last of them.

It's taken a while since I've been here,
but I'm resolved. What, didn't I print,
little piles of notes, slopes almost Sicilian?
Here is my friend:
Socks for comfort (now boys) will see later. Did they come?
The inner grocery had to take three sets of clips away.
Speaking to him of intricate family affairs,
I'm not what you think. Stay preconscious.
It's just the "flooding of the council." No need to feel afraid.

PASSIVE/AGGRESSIVE

We were driving along
at twenty-five miles an hour.
"Desperate" wants to know
how the angle tree has went. Or we now
can live over a wombat factory,
said the woman coming in to see him
about something.

And I was like,
a beautiful little tree, or lake.
Just the sandwiches now,
we'll look at the rest later
when you're out of time . . .
Oh yeah? *Oh, yeah*. That's it.
The water has swirled away to a
secret hiding place deep within earth.

Timid thing
out hitting the sun,
get me some peas . . . You're going tomorrow,

ribald headache misjudged, gray drunkard.
Lost vagrants unfold scrolls of pity.
I don't care how big his cock is, I'd . . . Oh, hullo, Marge.
Shredded any cumulus yesterday?
A sinister joy overtakes us.
Everybody has a body, that's why they're called everybody.
The affluent strapped to an accordion,
just as crazy in Baltimore and Point Reyes.
Something I don't remember eating:
the Mother Hubbard ship.
You seemed to be going good down there.

The very tegument strained, shuddering,
causing it to wobble: more dribs
than drabs, what summer
is supposedly about, more fluid, even.
He had spelling issues
but most of all, loved the country,
demented servitor, and what that person wants,
and what that person wanted.

What others said, as some went about their business,
isn't known.
Growing along the ridge, the condition of his parade
can't know.

Roger, sir, she meant it for only a little while. ROGER.

And when the ducks came squawking

back, one by one, you felt it was your responsibility.

The floral canopy dragged reproachfully, or so it seemed.

When lunch arrived you filled up on tea and goat cheese.

DAYS OF 1948

Friends of the deceased pole-vault toward us.
That's creepy. Not to be infiltrated, his pastures
stretch to the moon, the old place. Besides which
he kept telling us how nice we were, and that
was something. Was it in the old house
on the wires? Thanksgiving earlier,
with all the folks you've loved for years,
vagabond days, nights of mystery?
Yes boys, that's where my money goes.

Do you solemnly participate now,
where the tide is? Boink I love you.
Is that what you heard about him
that lets you distinguish between us
in the old opera house,
and you wake up screaming *"Arriba!"*

COCAINE FIENDS AND REEFER MADNESS

I downed a myosotis shot
and you came back bluer than before.

What at home should I do.
They don't want me inside.
Trouble me a blue barley twist
twisted the right way. You know how he likes it.
And when all is said and done the five and ten set off
for the coast one afternoon and were never seen again.
Hey you know how
lonely I always am because of you.
Now you can chuck it.
Forget New York the monstrous hillocks
like patterns of behavior we never looked for.
Hey it was spooky the way they curved in,
climbing for another time if all was well
as surely it must be, Mom and Dad.
It was the wizard's fault, that's what I say.

DARK ALIBI

Saw it in some lowbrow bread-and-butter programmer—
enough excitement for one day, wondering what it was.
The question is whether or not there's any rain
falling from those clouds.

You're so clear here. You can't not go through with it now,
and what topics there are! A sexy scream penetrates the
intellectual pillow fight guaranteeing further delays,
hedging. I know this! We're not gonna pay for this!

Once a night at the safe side,
if you would well encounter it, it's so breezy and nice.
I'll do whatever it can,
and not do it on someone's time,
or end up in a commercial. That said,
an unidentified rescue ship isn't rushing up
the sleeves of one's tennis shirt. They may be stones.
Put some of the stuff right on there.

THE MAUVE NOTEBOOK

Say it enough times and it's August.
GEOFFREY G. O'BRIEN, "Three Years"

On a set you need bush rebels,
that numbing little chair while passing.
If we knock 'em out
seven precincts are going to show up.
It looks like you don't need oil.
I think it'll be fine.
Did she think that might be good,
or for the man who listens to it,
nothing to be done or thought,
(suction pending)?

Or for the man who listens to it,
an abrupt yawn, history or the other.
Home economics. Dr. Singalong
can't find his way back.
I don't know about that, but
at her lamps do you still see
the awkward ceremony, too serious?

Leave it that way, imperfect start beyond
where I was going.
Prison outside the perpetual sonata,
the only anxiety,
since you wonder what they don't do,
from your red zero heart page
waiting to touch your face.

Although they know about it and
it literally doesn't exist,
no, stay up and go to sleep,
unless it falls on the right side of the brain
positioned for so many forgeries,
moon nugget . . .

I don't cut 'em any slack.
Assault on a clean front,
that's a lot to be turning into.

These residents, they start throwing 'em early.
Continue to open your door to mud!

Take the noon balloon to Rangoon,
gutta percha academy,
to the place of ice cream,

because, really, what difference does it make?
When it was time you went home.
Tears and flowers,

see how dirty your hands are.
We had a lovely dime.
Soon it will be seven I ask you.

EVENING AND ELSEWHERE

Say not the struggle naught availeth.
Soon you'll be out of here,
but hey you know what?
Freedom is a pin in the ass.

This middle quartet, my business card—
all is nice. The fucking sun,
yes, but way upstairs.
Place wax fruit on prepared cookie sheet.
But it was never connected.

Sans serif, spring is here, with poems
and bathtubs. Or shape our ornaments
more, which nobody can deny,
from American territories, and then you'll die.
Their blood through half a century
almost serene.

It can't have escaped your notice,
the musical consequences, some sort of a commitment.

Now we'll just travel more
for the thirteenth straight day,
like they had air conditioning.

They threw the book at him
under the bus, his salad cruiser
pleating intolerable morning effigies.
So yeah, duck for the oyster,
dig for the clam. And by the way,
it's velveteen, silly.

YCLEPT

It's not what you think, the power,
whether you want it or not:
a broken head and a lot of messy torsos.

The past should be more confident.
It has little to lose, and everything to gain.
She might have been sick long before.

Militants take note.
Thing is, no one saw it coming.
I cannot unwash my hand.

A lot can happen. Just last week
I like it that way, Bruce's ankle, eek,
the beautiful the beautiful.

You're up in the air, TV chef,
I am under the scenery. I got her into this,
and not just any debris, okay?

Save you eleven dollars every month
is all anyone still wants of it, and more
than these wildest animals.

ACKNOWLEDGMENTS

The author gratefully acknowledges the following publications and venues in which poems in *Commotion of the Birds* first appeared, sometimes in slightly different form: *The American Poetry Review*, *BOMB*, *Boston Review*, *Conjunctions*, *Critical Quarterly*, *Folder*, *Harper's Magazine*, *Intercourse*, *Literary Hub*, *London Review of Books*, *The New Republic*, *The New York Review of Books*, *The New Yorker*, *The Paris Review*, *PN Review*, *Poetry*, and *Tin House*.

"The Anxious Music," "Days of 1948," and "Rainbow Laundry" were published online in *50 Favorite US Poets: A Little American Anthology of New Writing*, edited by Douglas Messerli (Green Integer/Project for Innovative Poetry, 2016).

"The Mauve Notebook" first appeared in the Poetry Foundation's *PoetryNow* podcast series, co-produced by the WFMT Radio Network in Chicago, 2015.

"The Old Sofa" was commissioned by the Solomon R. Guggenheim Museum (New York) for its 2015 exhibition *Storylines: Contemporary Art at the Guggenheim*, in response to R.H. Quaytman's three-panel work *Point de Gaze, Chapter 23* (2011).

On the following pages, a stanza break occurs at the bottom of the page (not including pages on which the break is evident because of the regular stanzaic structure of the poem): 7, 9, 15, 18, 23, 32, 34, 38, 42, 43, 47, 49, 56, 59, 63, 72, 74, 79, 81, 92.

John Ashbery was born in Rochester, New York, in 1927. He earned degrees from Harvard and Columbia, and went to France as a Fulbright Scholar in 1955, living there for much of the next decade. His many collections of poetry include *Breezeway* (2015), *Quick Question* (2012), *Planisphere* (2009) and *Notes from the Air: Selected Later Poems* (2007), which was awarded the 2008 International Griffin Poetry Prize. *Self-Portrait in a Convex Mirror* (1975) won the three major American prizes—the Pulitzer, the National Book Award, and the National Book Critics Circle Award—and an early book, *Some Trees* (1956) was selected by W. H. Auden for the Yale Younger Poets Series. The Library of America published the first volume of his collected poems in 2008. A two-volume set of his collected translations from the French (poetry and prose) was published in 2014. Active in various areas of the arts throughout his career, he has served as executive editor of *Art News* and as art critic for *New York Magazine* and *Newsweek*; he exhibits his collages at the Tibor de Nagy Gallery (New York). He taught for many years at Brooklyn College (CUNY) and Bard College, and in 1989–90 delivered the Charles Eliot Norton lectures at Harvard. He is a member of the American Academy of Arts and Letters (receiving its Gold Medal for Poetry in 1997) and the American Academy of Arts and Sciences, and was a chancellor of the Academy of American Poets from 1988 to 1999. The winner of many prizes and awards, both nationally and internationally, he has received two Guggenheim Fellowships and was a MacArthur Fellow from 1985 to 1990; recently, he received the Medal for Distinguished Contribution to American Letters from the National Book Foundation (2011) and a National Humanities Medal, presented by President Obama at the White House (2012). His work has been translated into more than twenty-five languages. He lives in New York. Additional information is available in the "About John Ashbery" section of the Ashbery Resource Center's website, a project of The Flow Chart Foundation, www.flowchartfoundation.org/arc.